SCHIRMER'S LIBRARY
OF MUSICAL CLASSICS

Vol. 2125

The Indispensable
DEBUSSY
Collection

19 Famous Piano Pieces

ISBN 978-1-4950-7159-1

G. SCHIRMER, *Inc.*

DISTRIBUTED BY

 HAL•LEONARD®

7777 W. BLUEMOUND RD. P.O. BOX 13819 MILWAUKEE, WI 53213

www.musicsalesclassical.com
www.halleonard.com

CONTENTS

Children's Corner

Doctor Gradus ad Parnassum

Claude Debussy

Animato ma non troppo

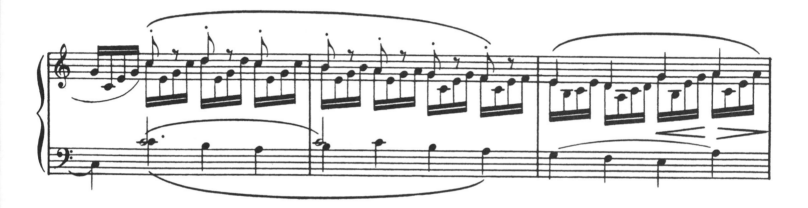

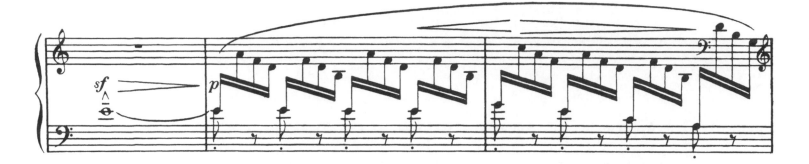

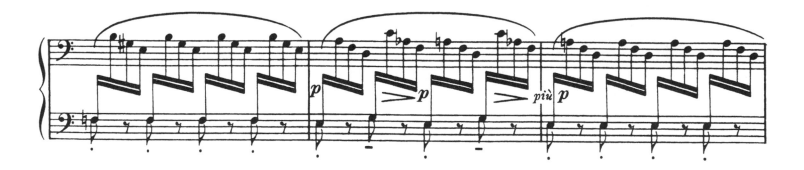

Poco ritenuto　　　　// **a Tempo**

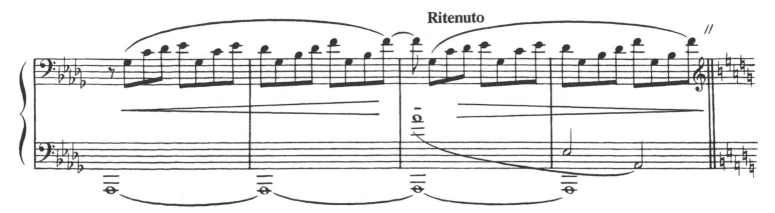

Tempo I

pp
pp

pp

pp
cre - scen - do

Poco a poco animando

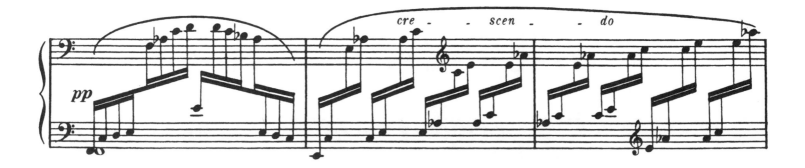

f

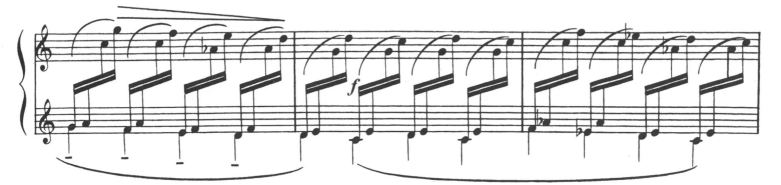

Molto animato

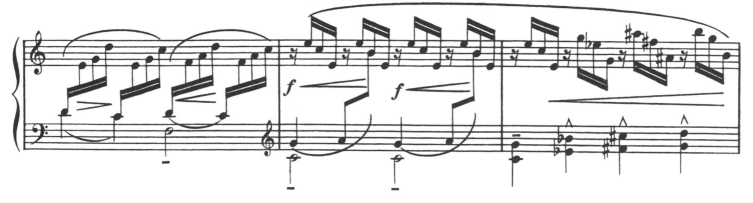

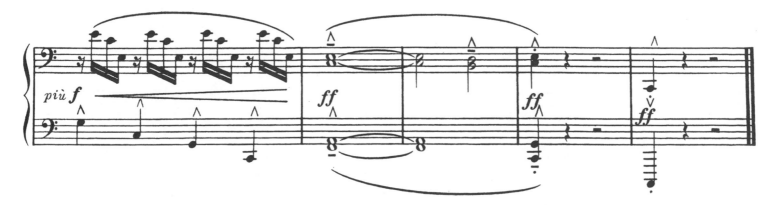

Children's Corner
Jimbo's Lullaby

Claude Debussy

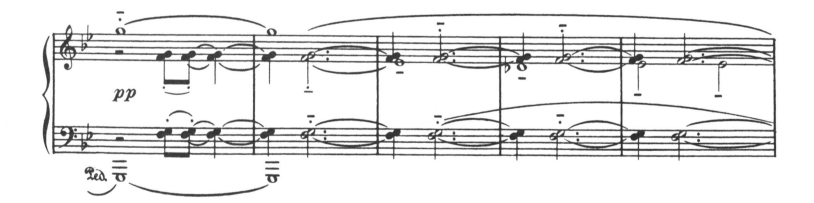

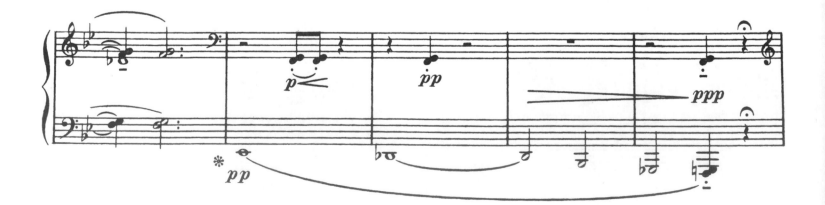

poco in fuori

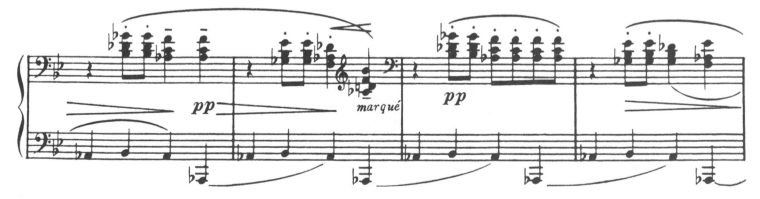

Poco più mosso

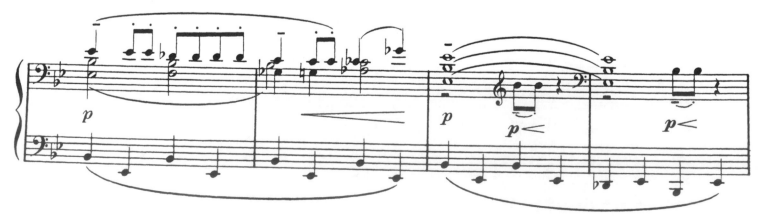

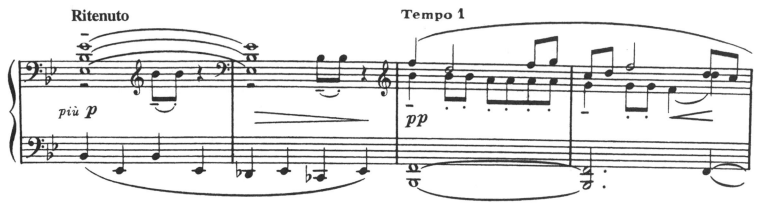

Ritenuto

Tempo 1

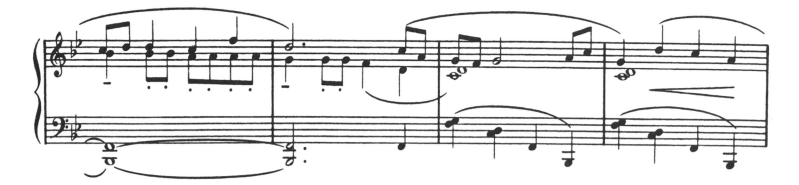

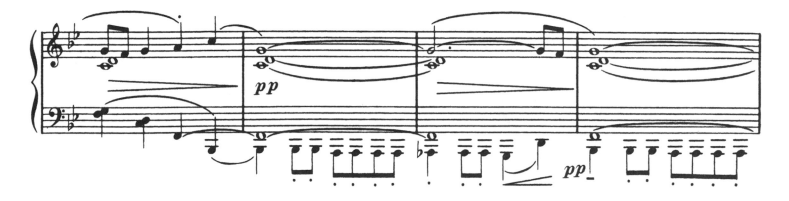

Sempre pp e senza rallentare

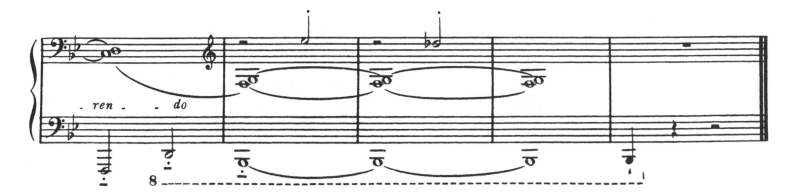

Children's Corner
Serenade for the Doll

Claude Debussy

Allegretto ma non troppo

leggero e grazioso

la m.s. un poco in fuori

la m.d. un poco in fuori

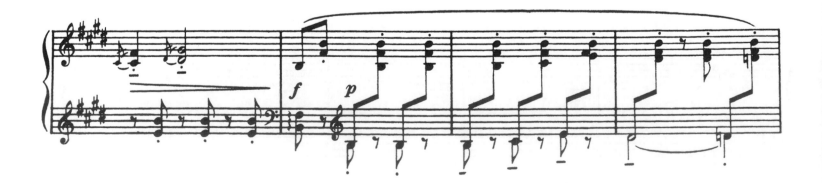

poco   a   poco   crescendo

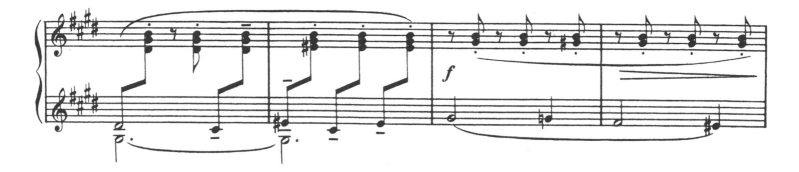

Poco ritenuto

Tempo I

14

Rallentare

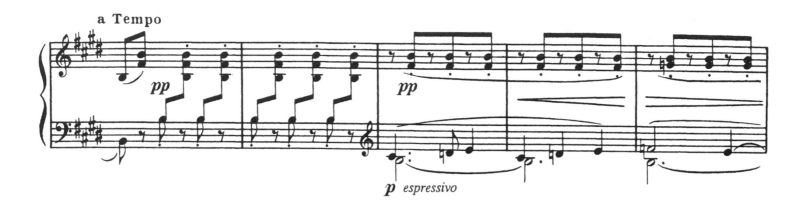

a Tempo

pp

pp

p espressivo

Poco animando

p

p

Tempo I

Senza rallentare

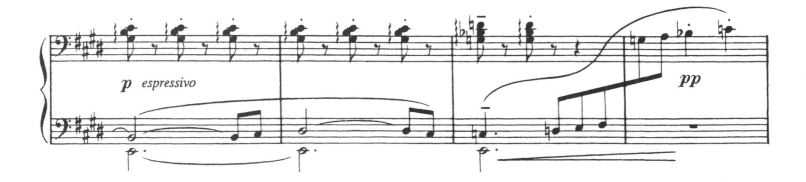

Children's Corner
The snow is dancing

Claude Debussy

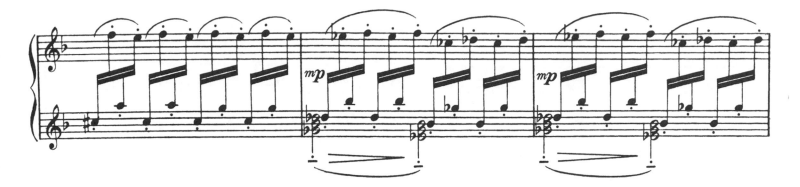

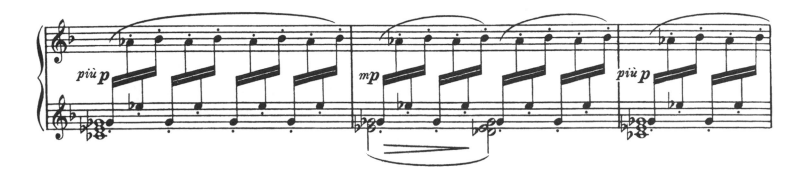

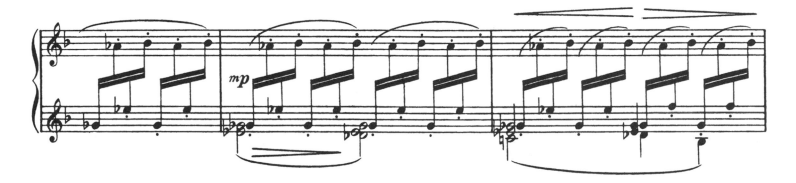

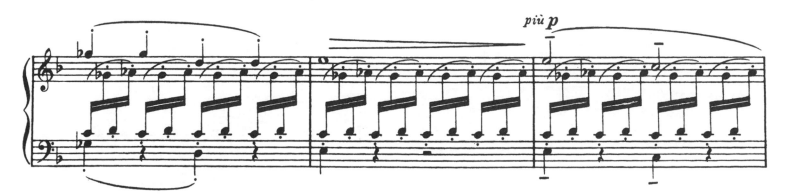

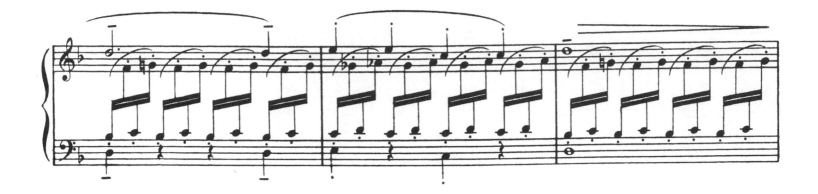

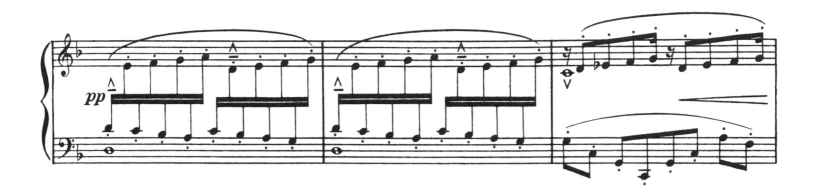

Poco rallentare

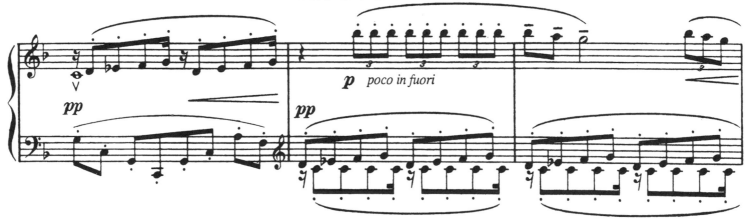

A tempo

Poco rallentare

A tempo

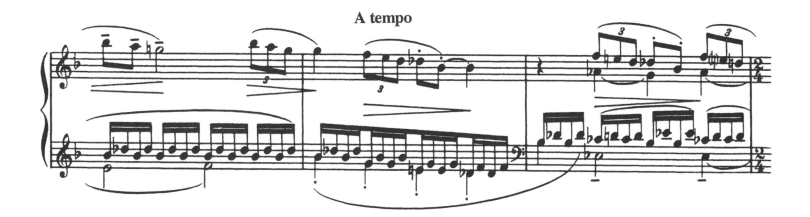

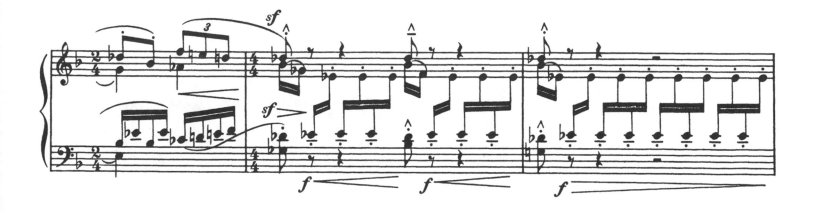

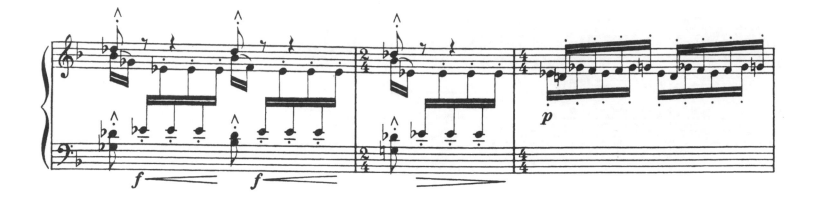

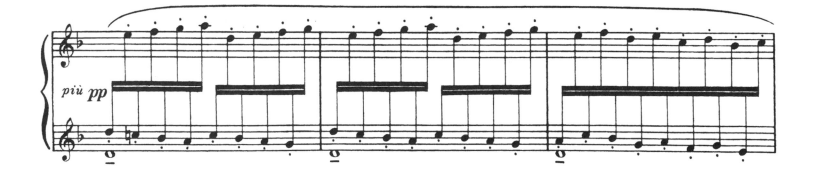

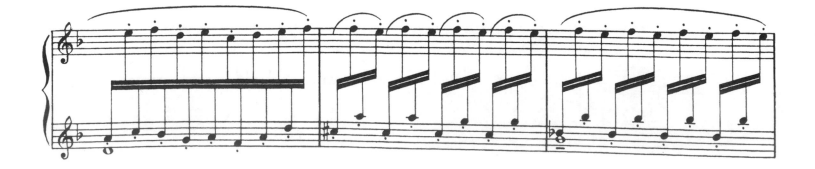

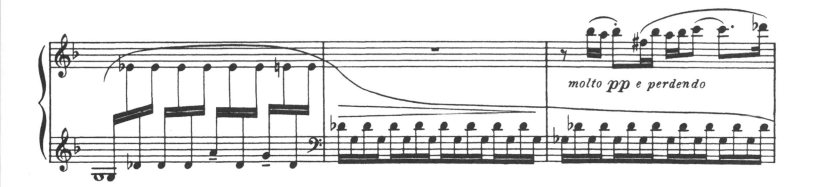

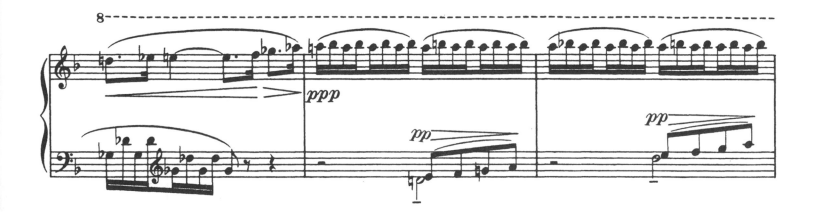

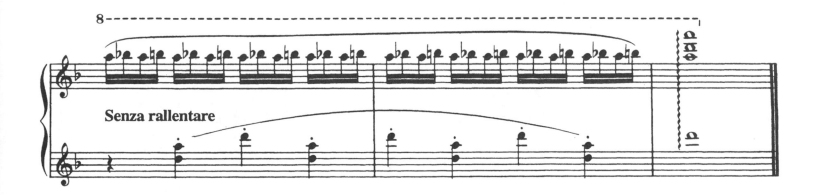

Children's Corner
The little Shepherd

Claude Debussy

Molto moderato

Più mosso

A tempo · **Rallentare**

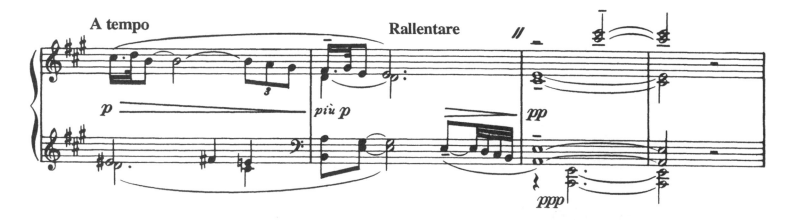

A tempo

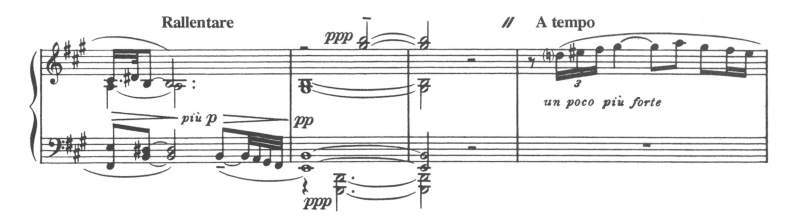

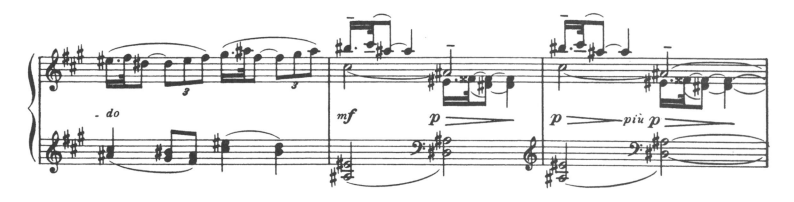

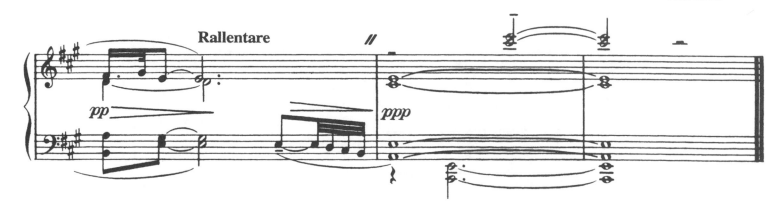

Children's Corner
Golliwogg's cake walk

Claude Debussy

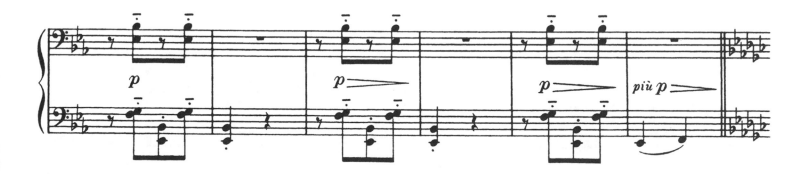

Poco meno mosso

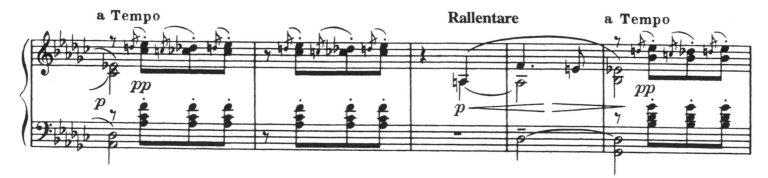

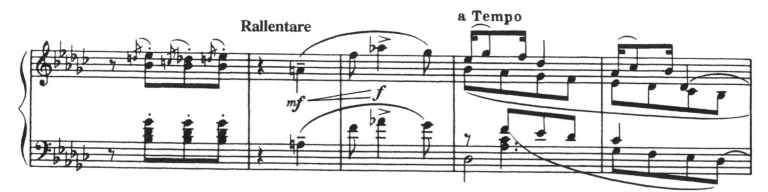

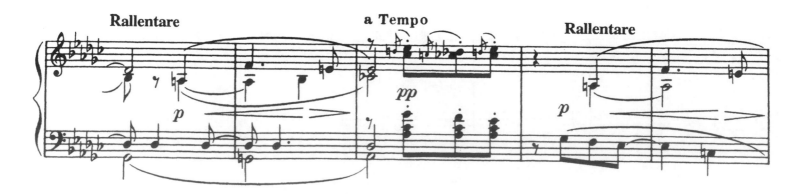

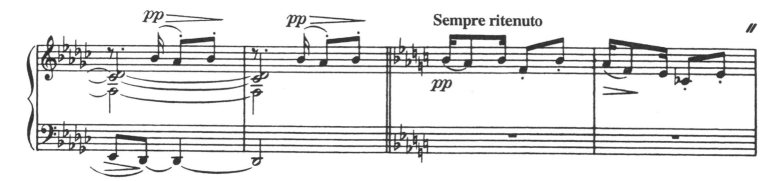

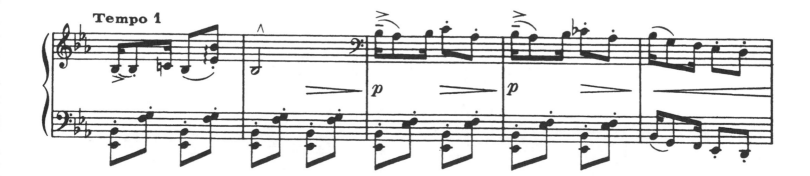

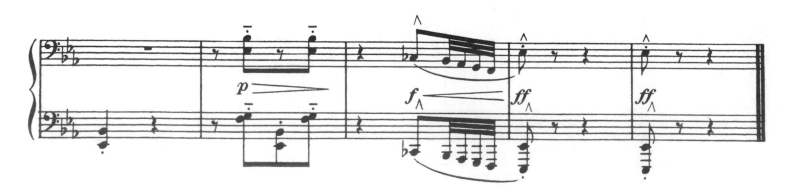

Deux Arabesques
Première Arabesque

Claude Debussy

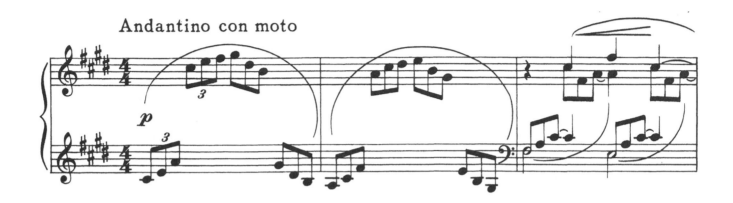

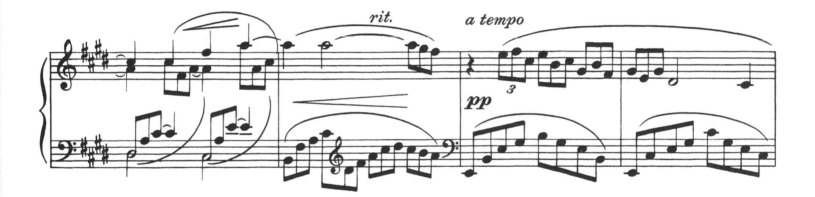

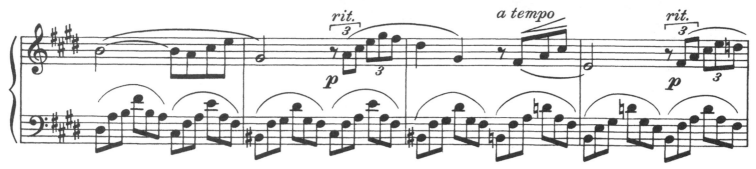

Tempo rubato *(un peu moins vite) (somewhat slower)*

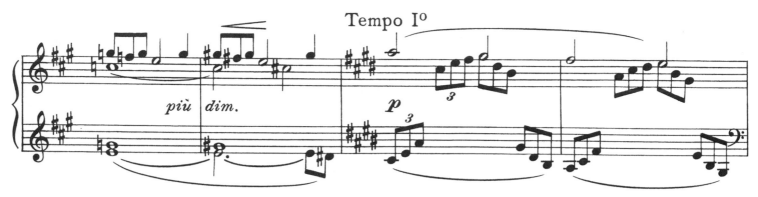

Deux Arabesques

Deuxième Arabesque

Claude Debussy

Allegretto scherzando

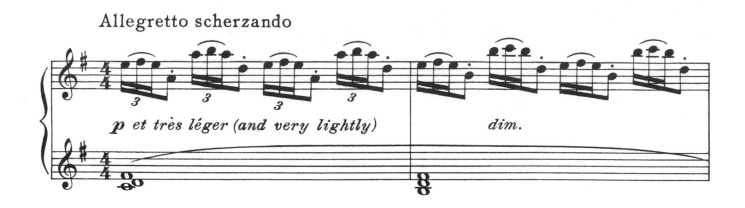

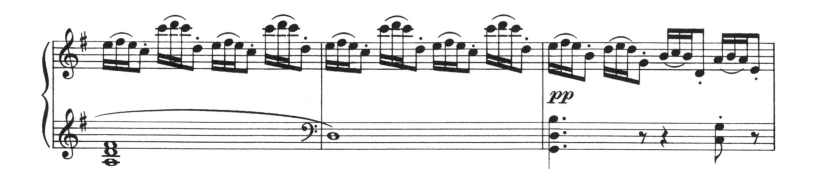

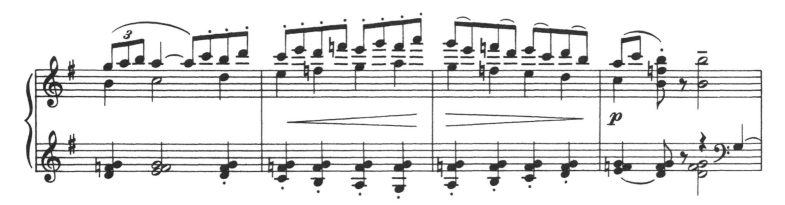

Pour le Piano
Prélude

Claude Debussy

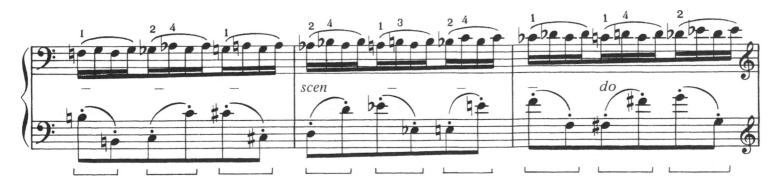

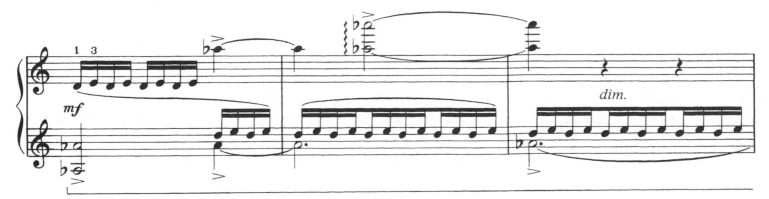

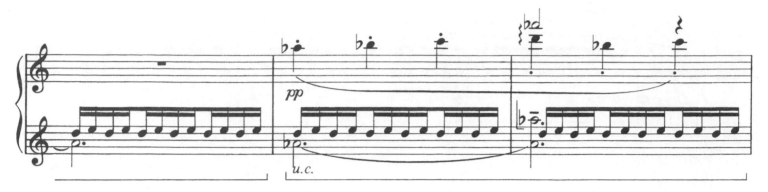

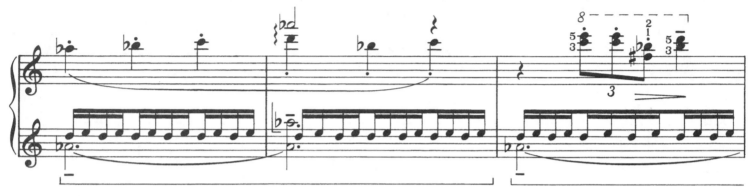

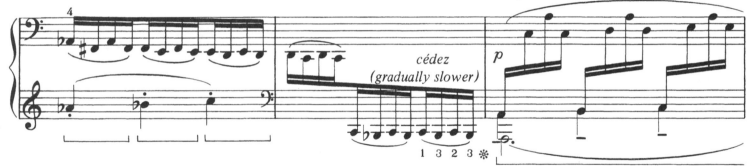

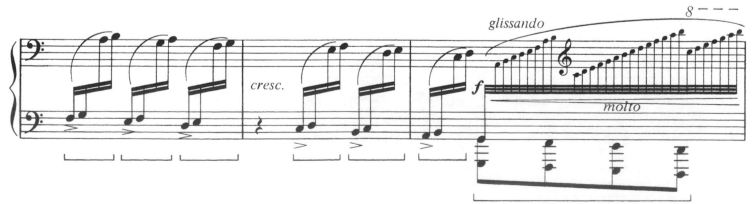

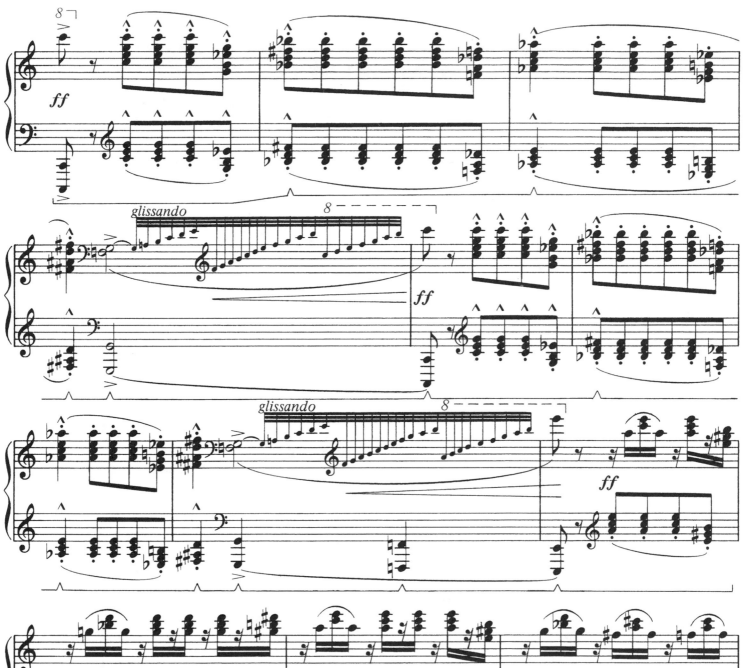

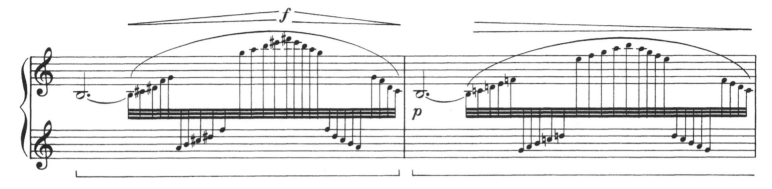

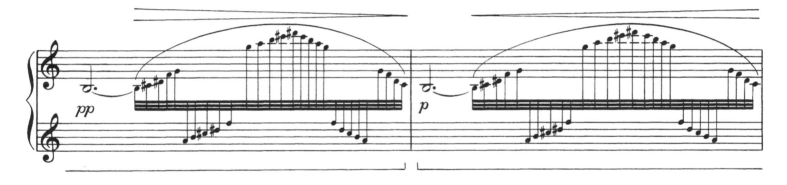

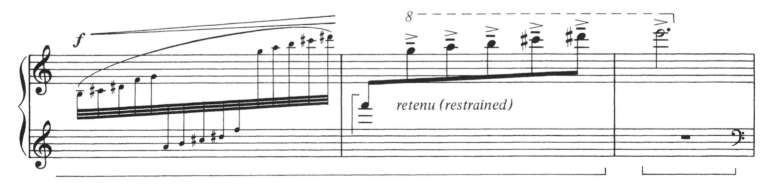

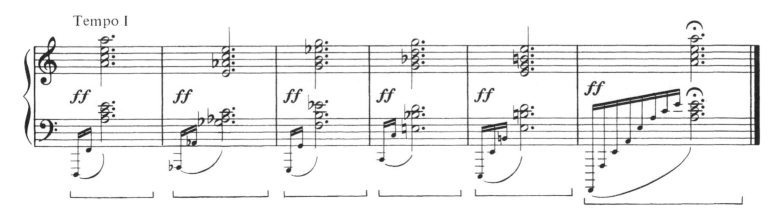

Pour le Piano
Sarabande

Claude Debussy

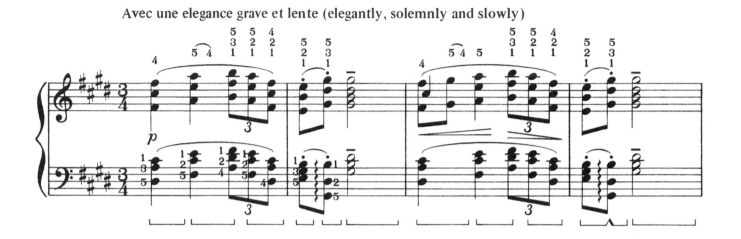

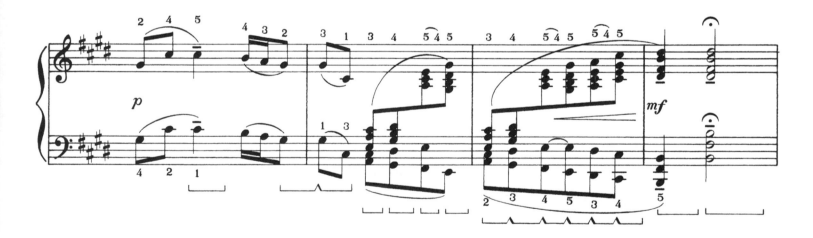

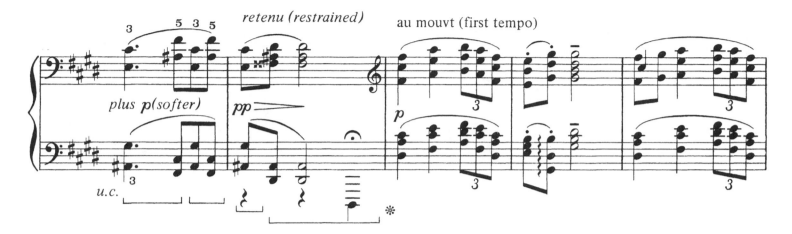

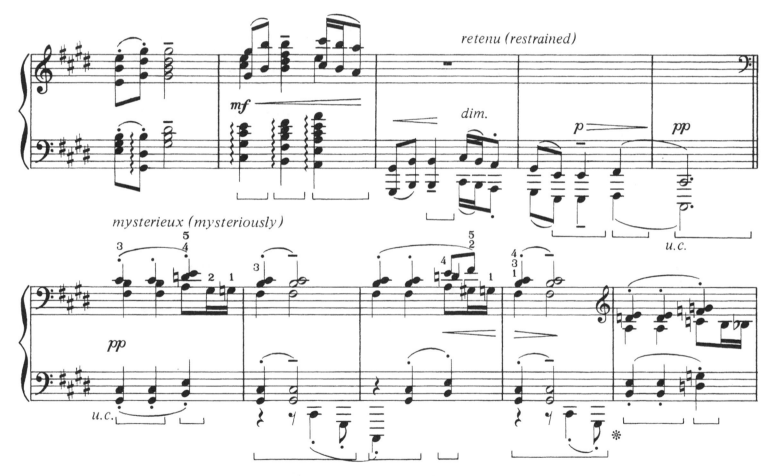

56

animez un peu (gradually faster)
très soutenu (very sustained)

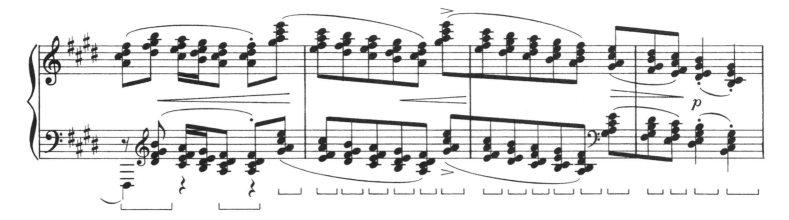

au mouvt (first tempo)

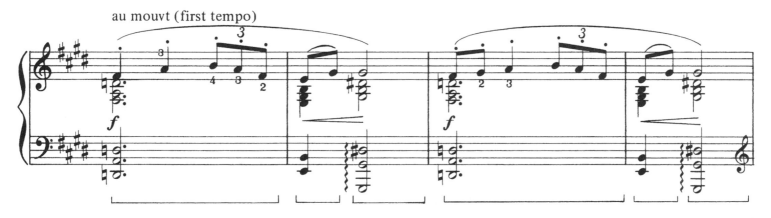

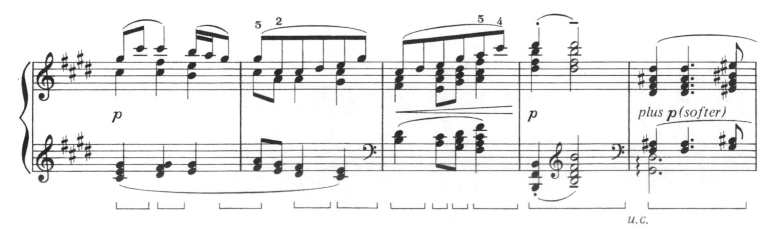

u.c.

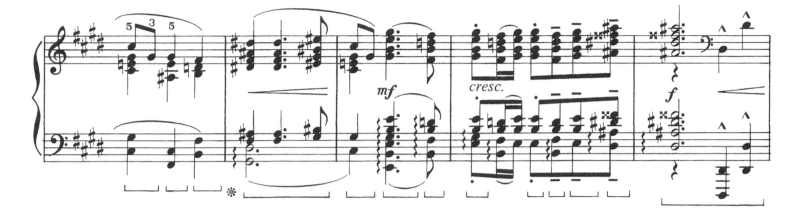

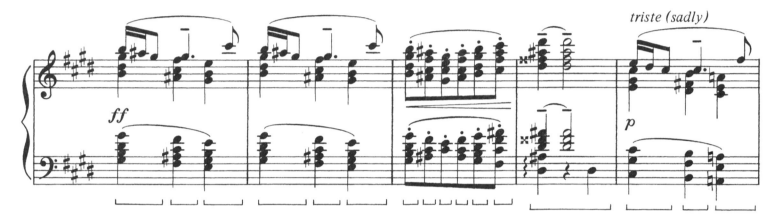

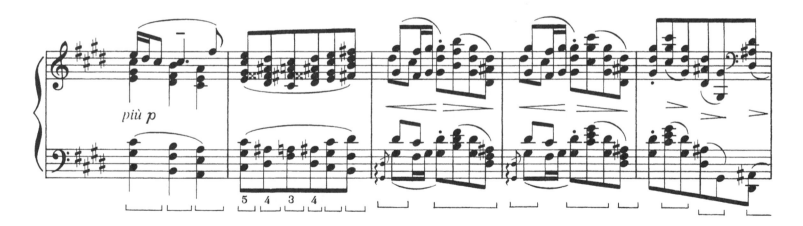

Le petit nègre

Claude Debussy

Allegro giusto

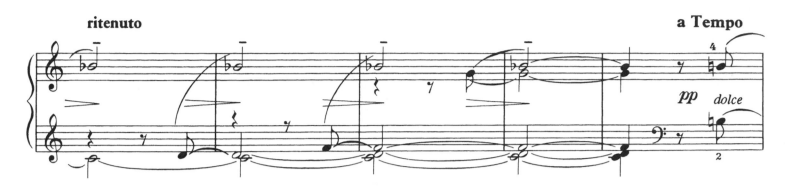

ed espressivo

Ritenuto

cresc.

f

a Tempo

Préludes, Livre I

La Cathédrale engloutie

Claude Debussy

Profondément calme (Dans une brume doucement sonore)

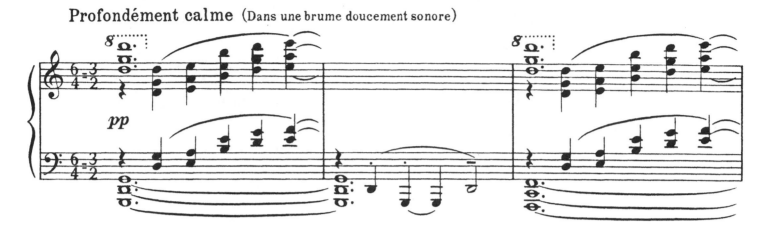

*) **Doux et fluide**

*) Debussy, in his piano-roll recording (Welte-Mignon), played measures 7–12 and 22–83 in double speed.

Peu à peu sortant de la brume

sempre pp   *p marqué pp*

p marqué pp   *p*   *marqué*

Augmentez progressivement (Sans presser)

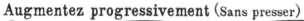

f   *più f*

Sonore sans dureté

sff   *ff*

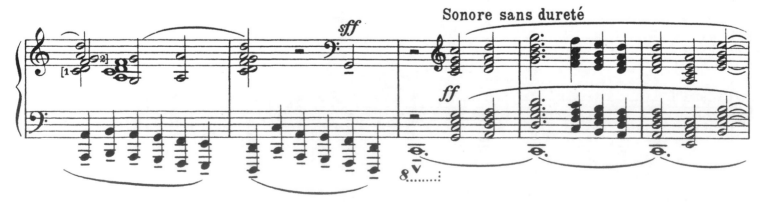

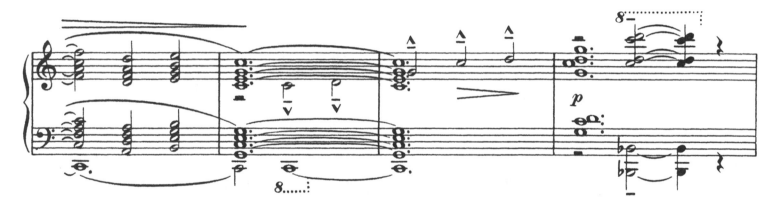

Un peu moins lent (Dans une expression allant grandissant)

pp expressif et concentré

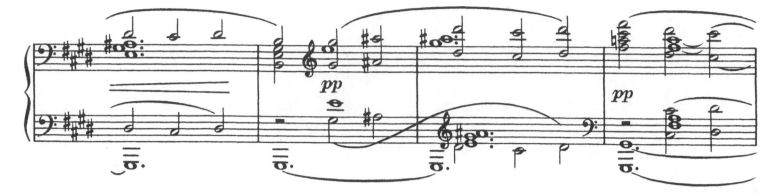

au Mouvement

Préludes, Livre I

Des pas sur le neige

Claude Debussy

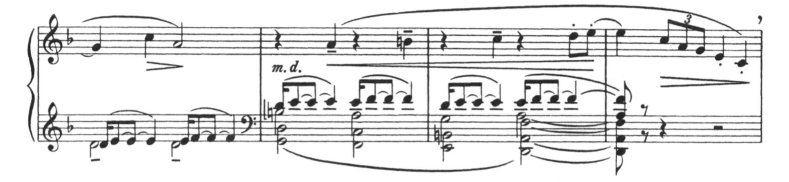

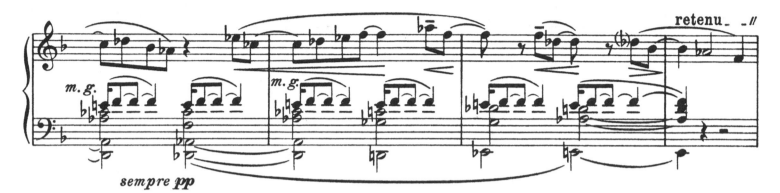

Préludes, Livre I
La fille aux cheveux de lin

Claude Debussy

Très calme et doucement expressif (♩=66)

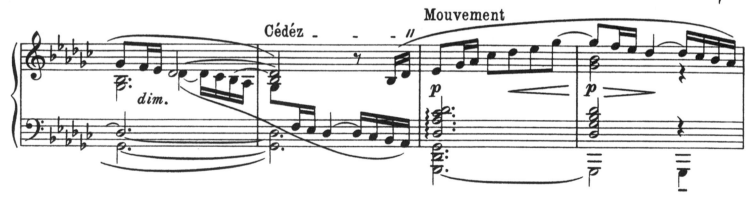

Cédéz _ _// Mouvement (sans lourdeur)

Cédéz _ _// au Mouvement   *très doux*

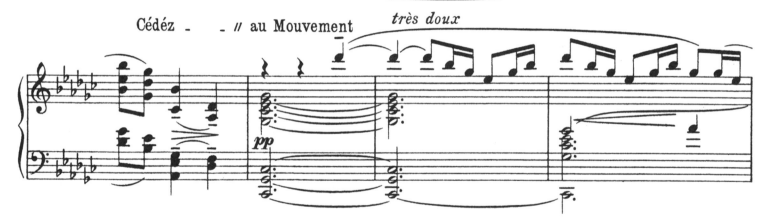

Murmuré et en retenant peu à peu

Préludes, Livre I

Minstrels

Claude Debussy

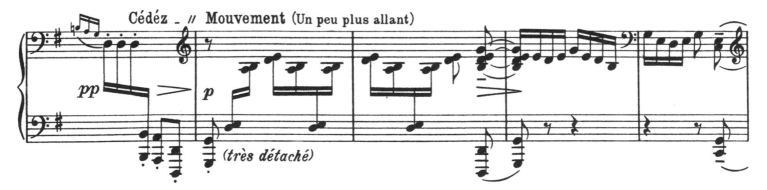

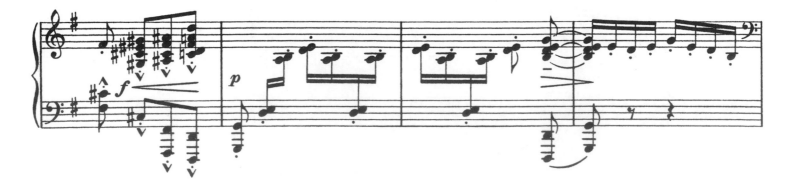

Hommage à S. Pickwick Esq. P. P. M. P. C.

Claude Debussy

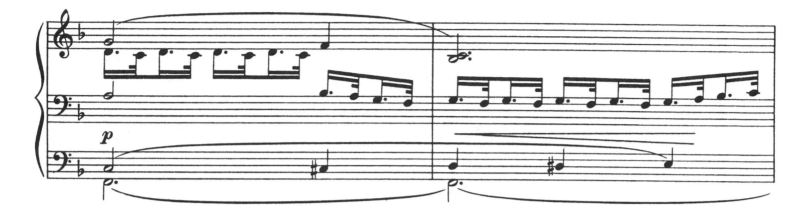

Animez peu à peu

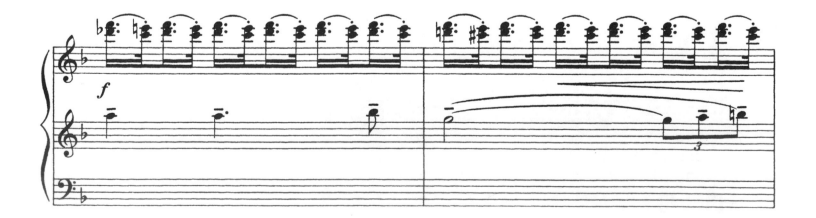

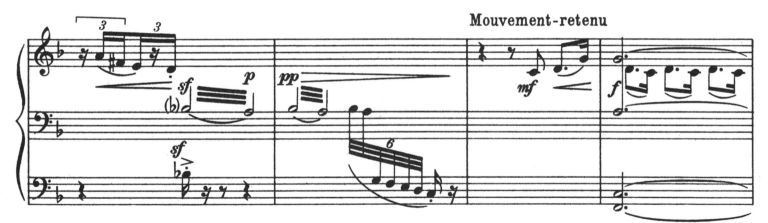

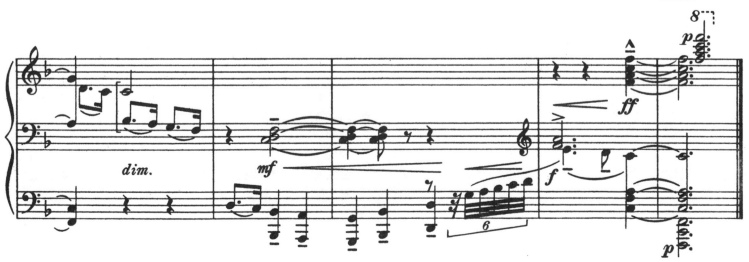

Suite bergamasque
Prélude

Claude Debussy

Moderato *(tempo rubato)*

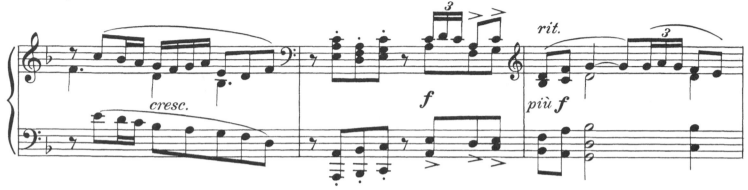

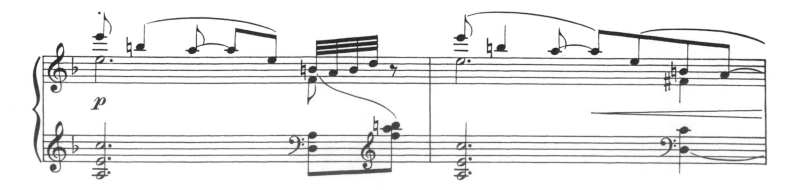

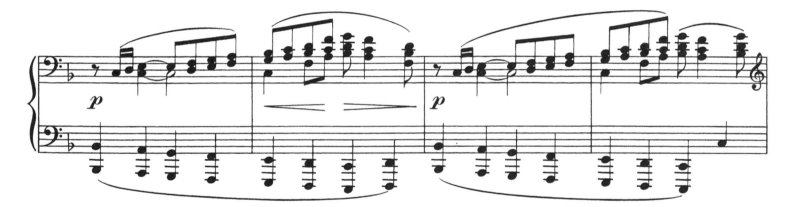

Suite bergamasque

Clair de lune

Claude Debussy

Andante *très expressif (very expressively)*

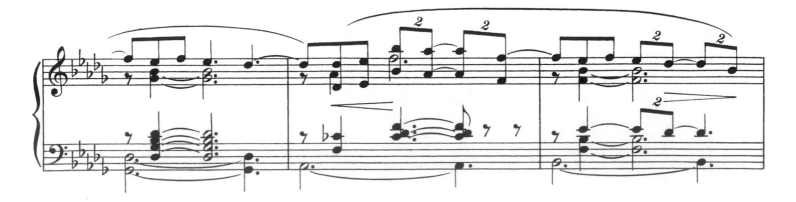

Tempo rubato

pp

peu à peu cresc. et animé (louder and livelier)

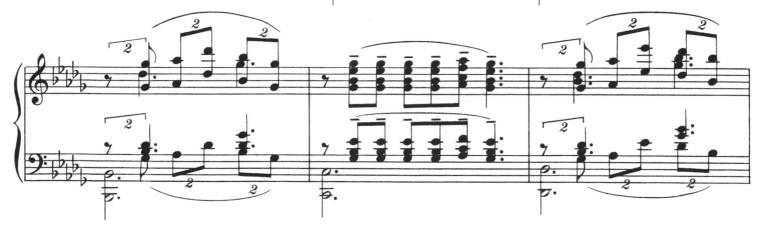

dim. molto

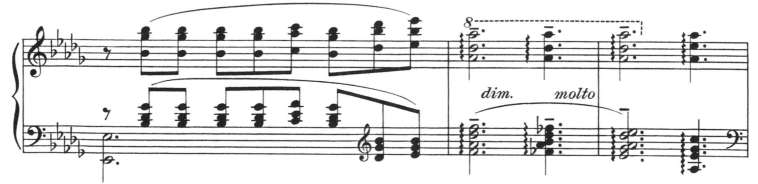

un poco mosso

pp

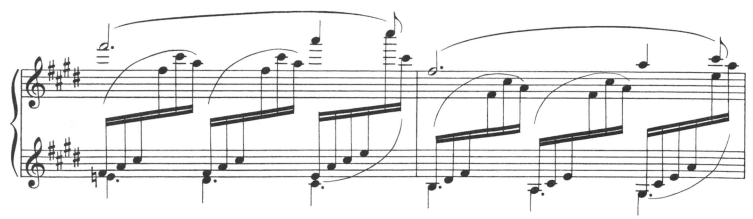

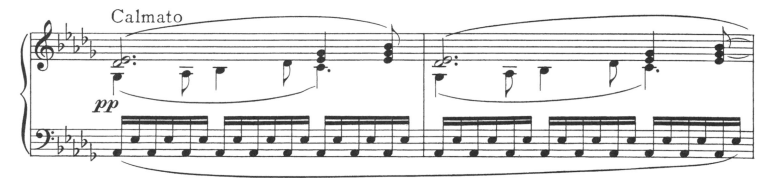

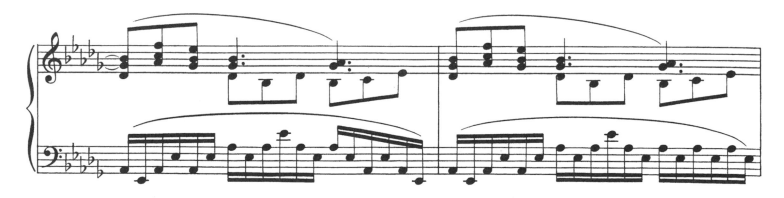

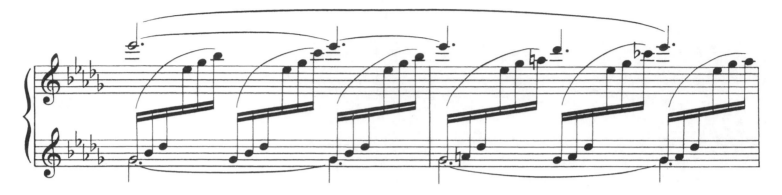

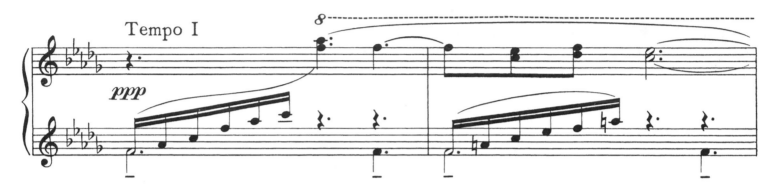

Tempo I

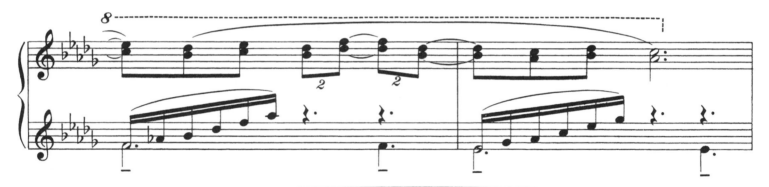

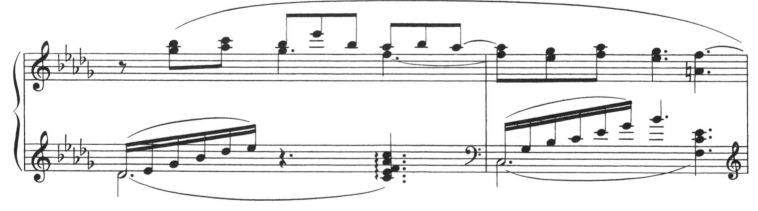

pp morendo jusqu'à la fin (more and more faint to the end)

Rêverie

Claude Debussy

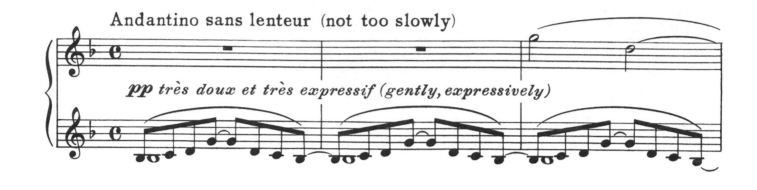

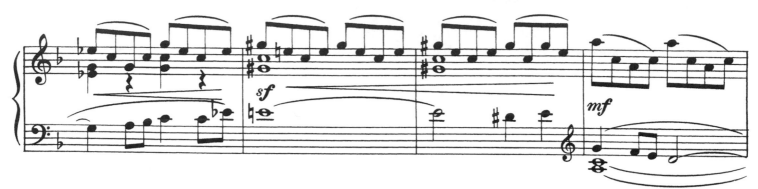

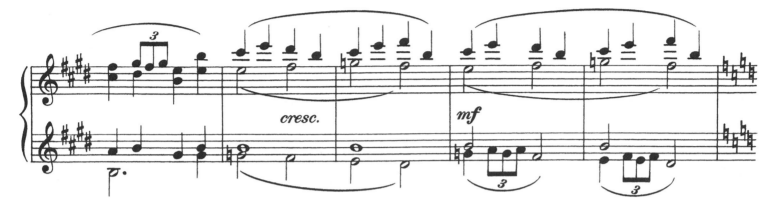